mel bay's

handbook for violin students

by frank zucco

© 1989 BY MEL BAY PUBLICATIONS, INC., PACIFIC, MO.

Bowing Signs

V - Up. Bow W.B. - Whole - Bow
⊓ - Down - Bow H.B. - Half Bow
Pt. - Point of Bow M-B. - Middle of Bow
U-B. - Upper Bow L - B. - Lower - Part of Bow
            N - Nut

To produce a clear even tone bow should - be moved in a straight-line parallel to the bridge at all - times

Sparing The Bow

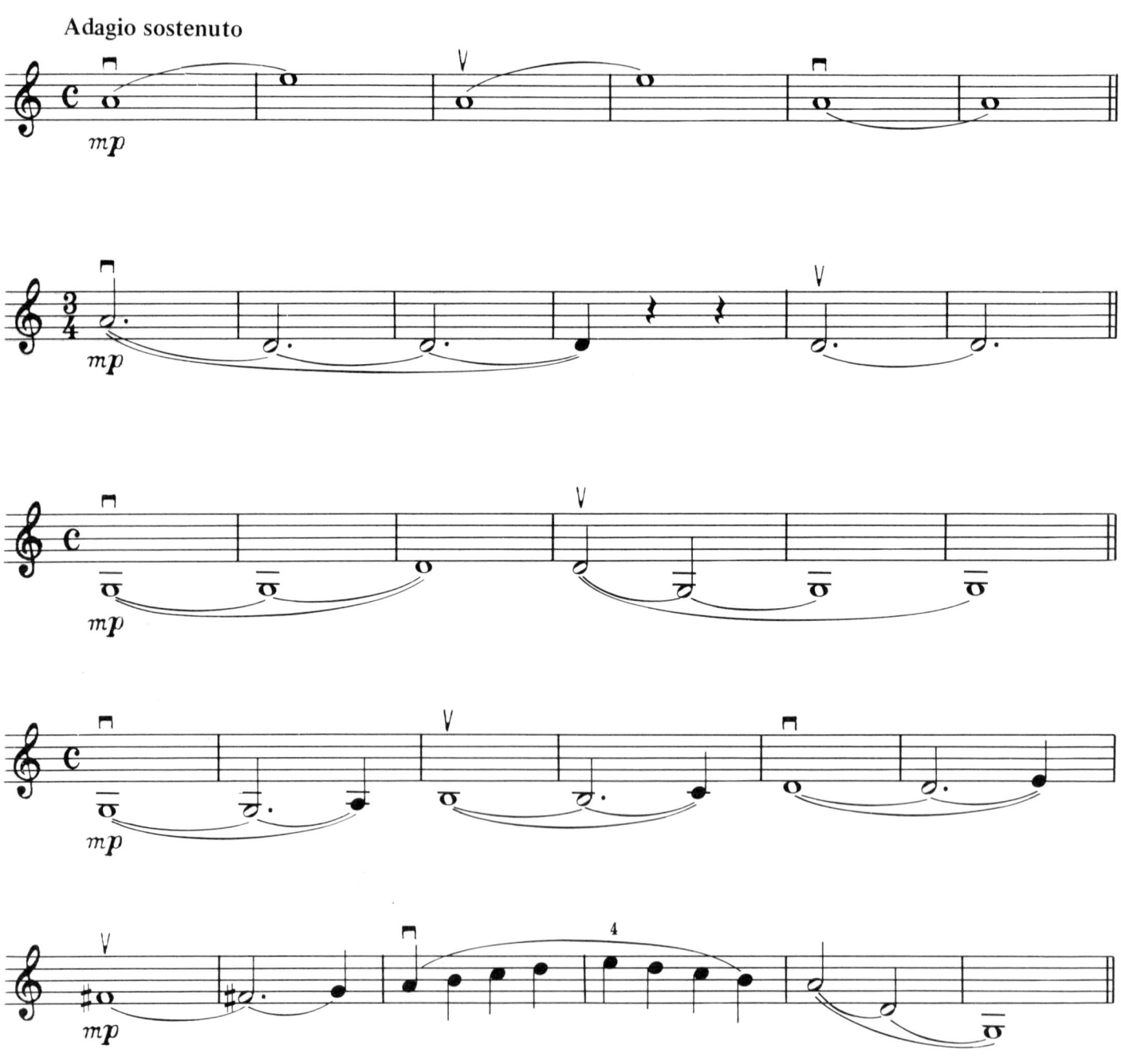

Bend the wrist slightly when approaching the bridge. Mastering the above studies will be time well spent.

Sustain the notes and spare the bow on the following examples.

3 and 4

The following examples 3 and 4 are played with the elbow remaining at one level. The wrist moves in an up and down vertical motion. Continue sparing the bow.

Abbreviation Marks

Oblique strokes which distinguish the eight sixteenth or thirty-second notes, when applied to the stem of a quarter half or any note, are equal to the longer note represented. Groups of notes are sometimes abbreviated as follows.

Examples

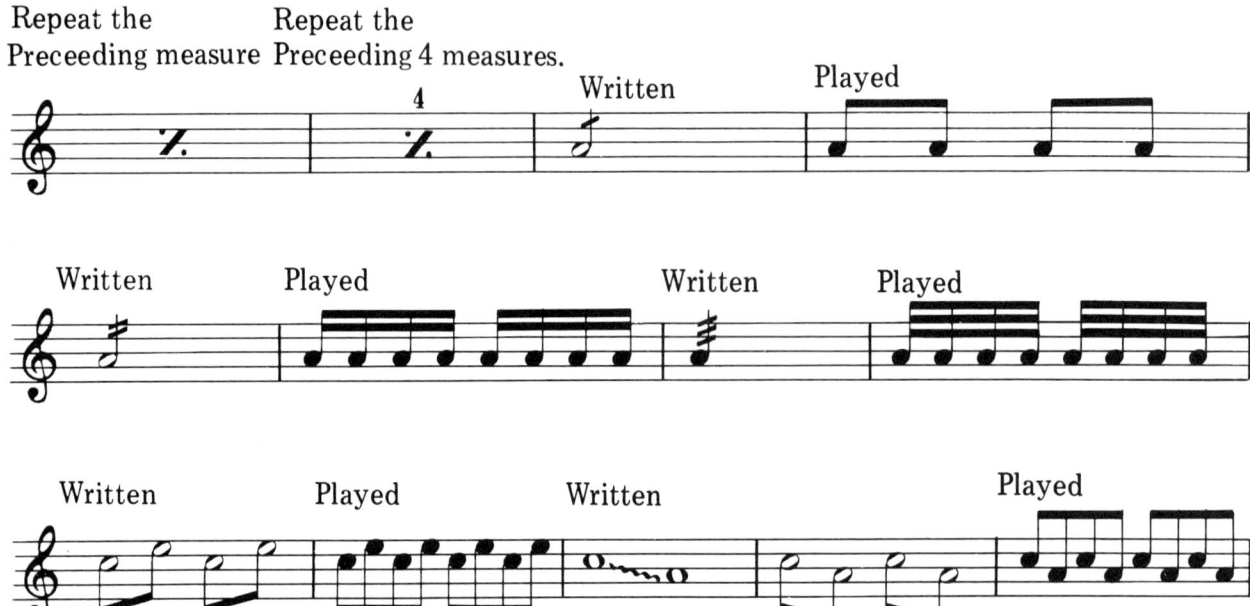

The sign called "the direct" (W) means to continue in the same manner, and at the same time, indicates the first note of each succeeding group

The Trill

Its sign is-tr-or-tr~~~~~~ It consists of a rapid alteration of the printed note, and the next note above, to the value of the printed note.
A trill generally ends with a turn, especially if it has the rhythmic value of a half note or more.

With a flexable wrist and light, even tone, practice the following as indicated below.
① MB ② UB ③ LB

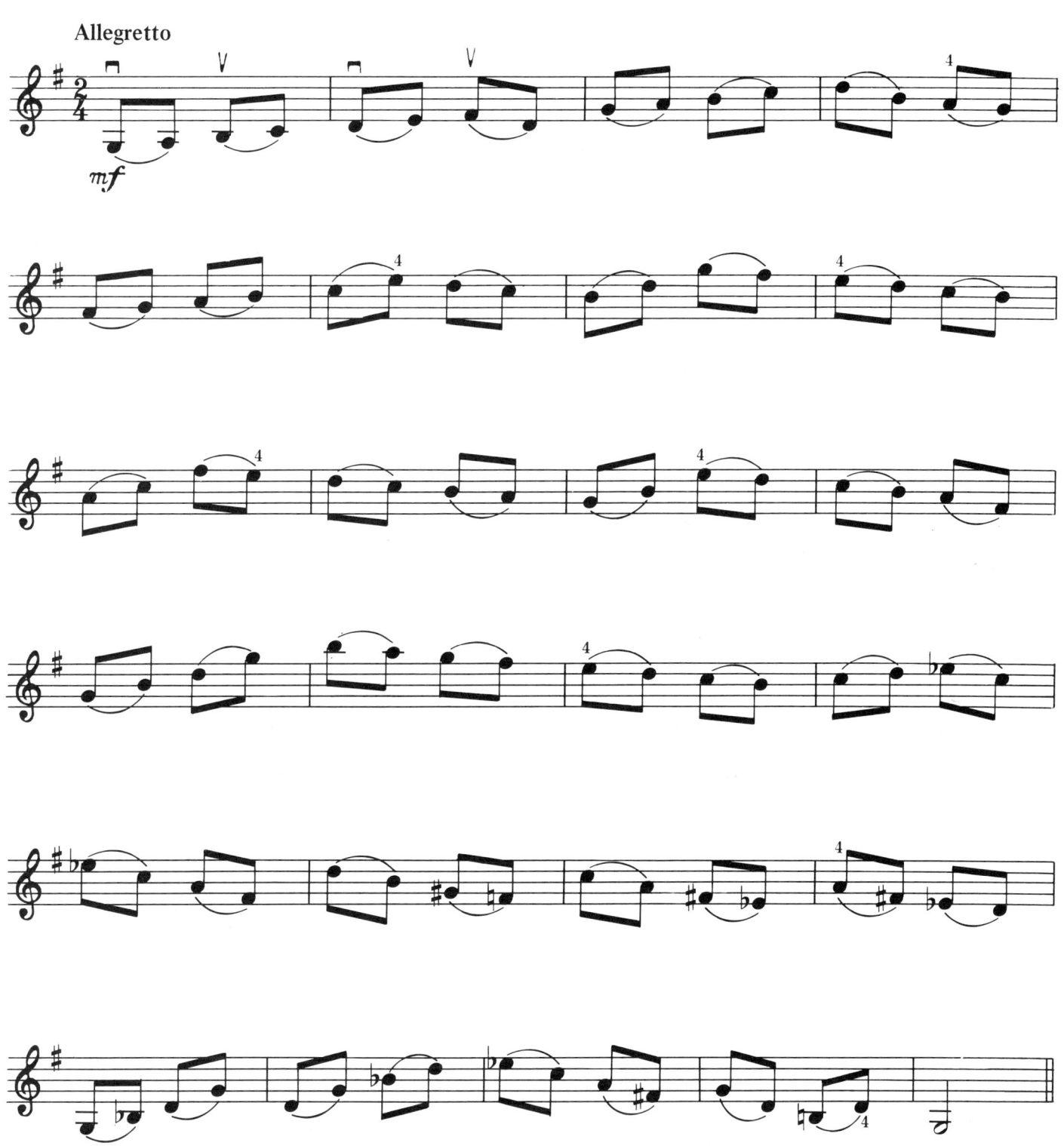

Saltato-or Bouncing The Bow

Start the bouncing at a slow tempo with a short and shallow well controlled bounce at the center of the bow. For increasing the speed, use shorter strokes and a well-relaxed wrist. The bow is not lifted from the string but jumps as a result of the natural spring of the stick.

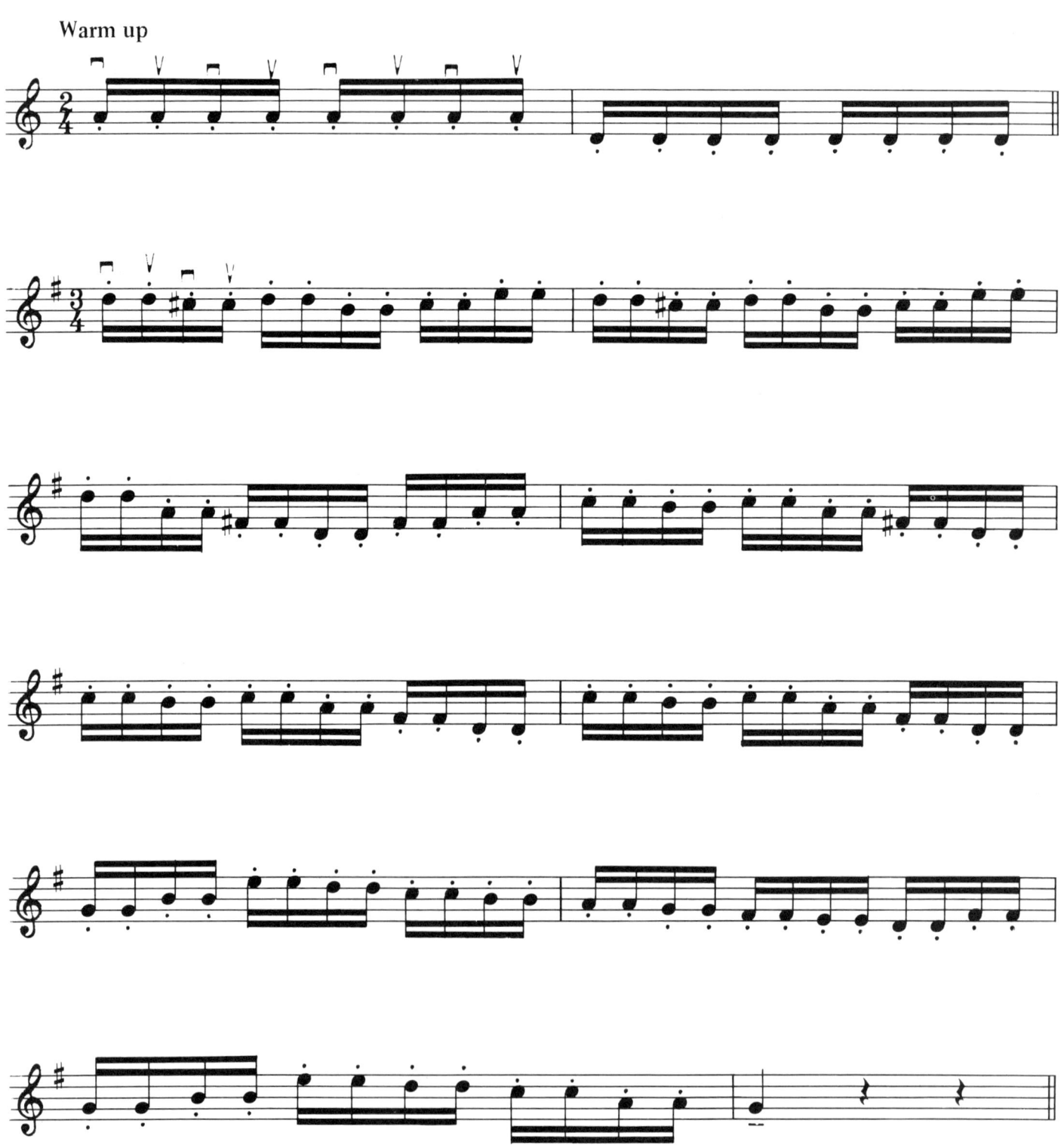

Begin by practicing the staccato stroke very slowly, all notes evenly and firmly accentuated with a free wrist, but without raising the bow, advance the tempo "A- Piacere."

The violin attained its present shape with four strings in the sixteenth century.

Bowing Continued

Check Point

Mastering the above bowing example will be time well spent.

Bowing - Continued

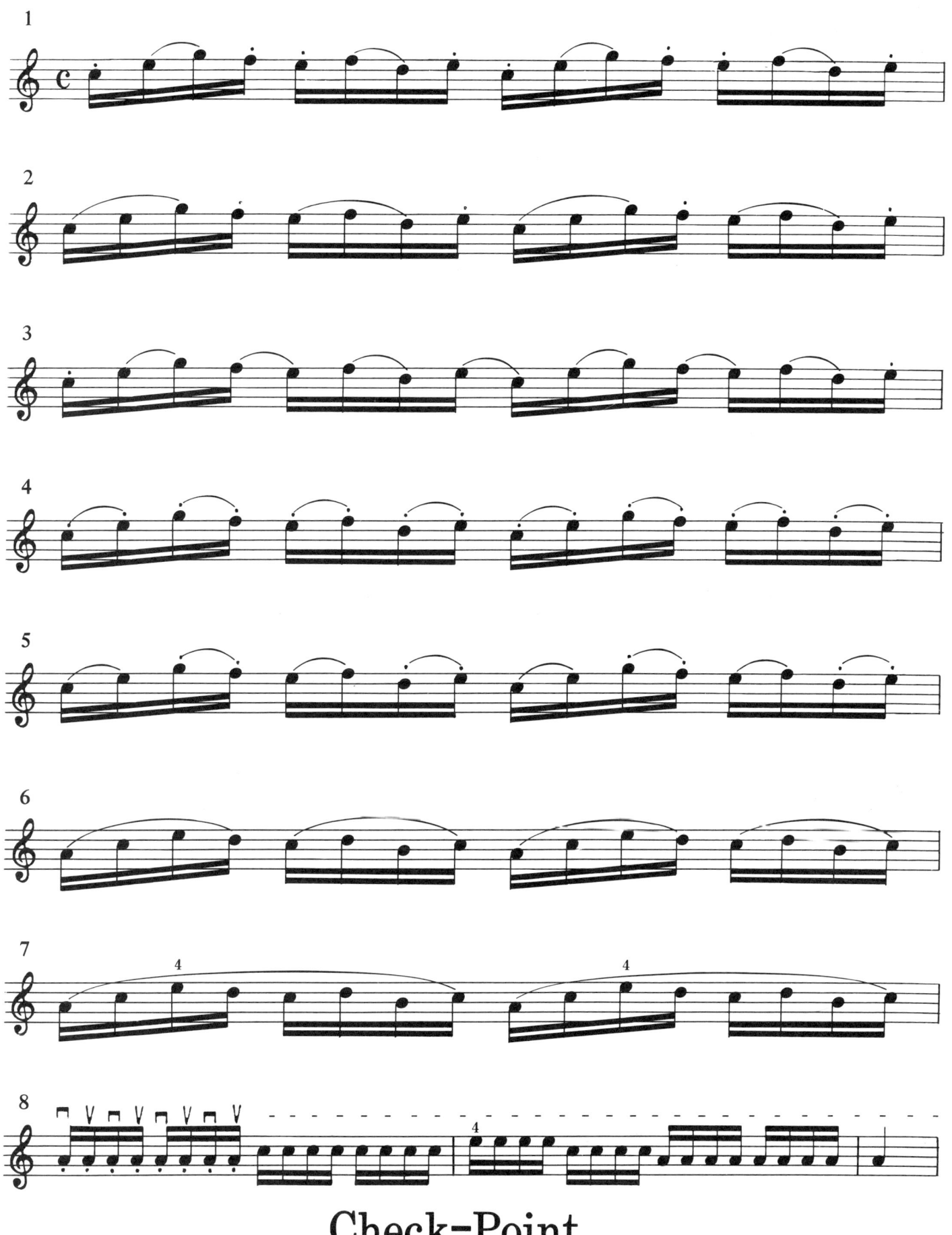

Check-Point

Ex. No 8 - Sultato - Jumping - Bouncing bow. The instructor could be a big help on the above subject.

An abreviated refresher approach to the third position check point
1 Hand position. Elbow well underneath the violin
2 Wrist straight, fingers curved over the fingerboard
3 The shifting (or sliding) motion is done by moving the forearm and hand up (do not bend the wrist). When moving back to the first position, reverse the procedure.
4 Do not change the formation of the hand when shifting (rule No 2)

Intonation Is Very Important

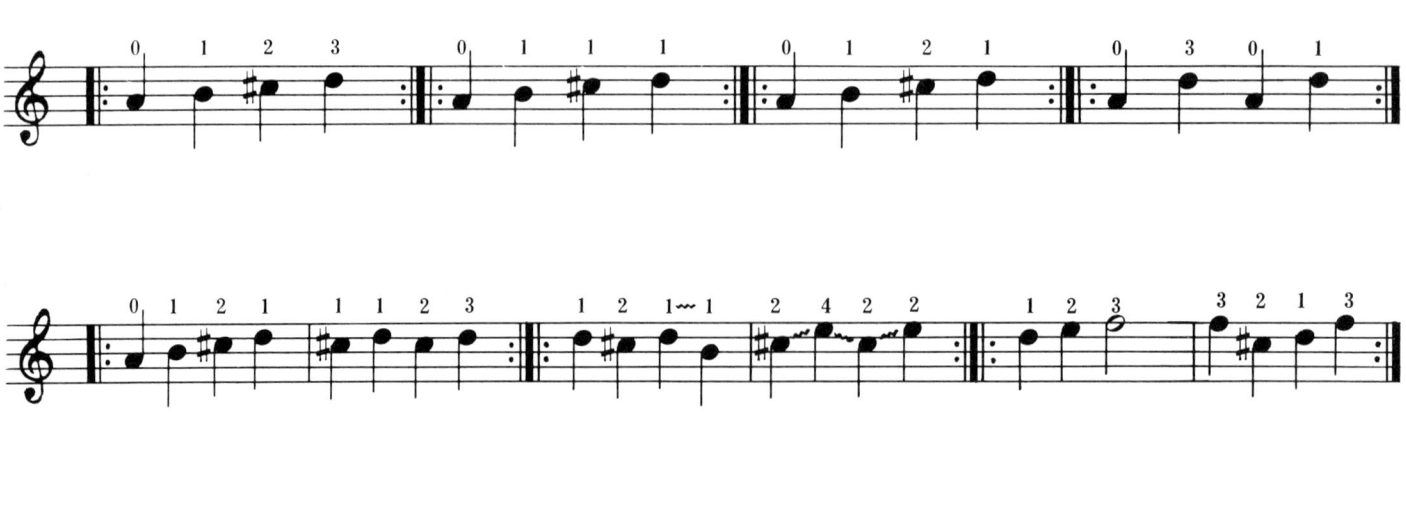

Third Position Continued

More About The Third Position

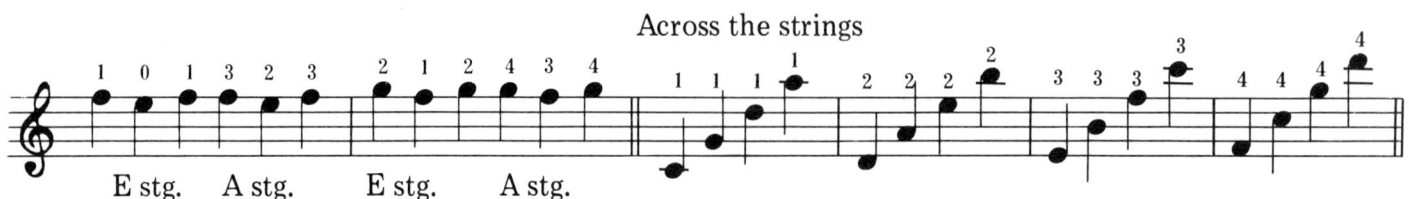

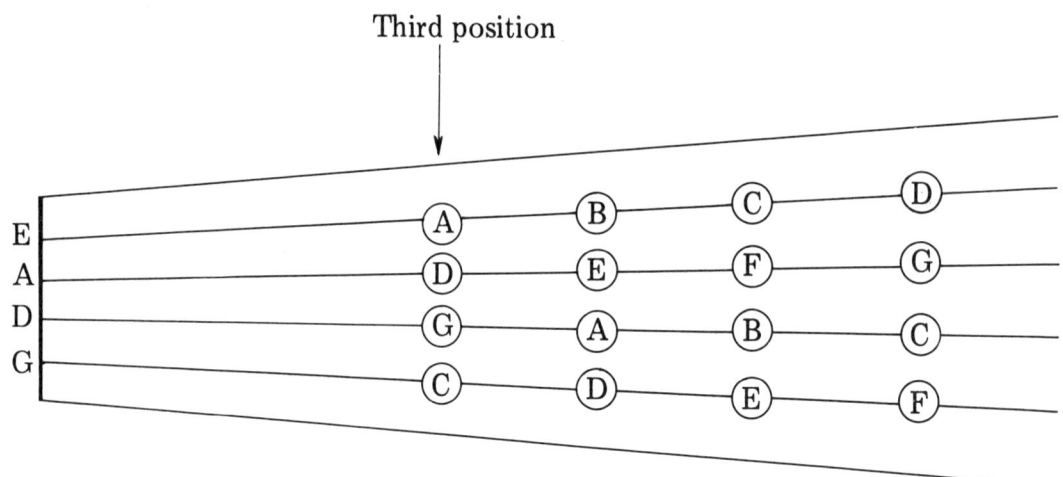

The Scale

A scale or tone ladder is a series or succession of tones arranged in regular order ascending or decending. There are many forms of scales in use, but we have to deal at present with the major-melodic-harmonic-natural normal and the hungarian (gypsy) minor.

C major

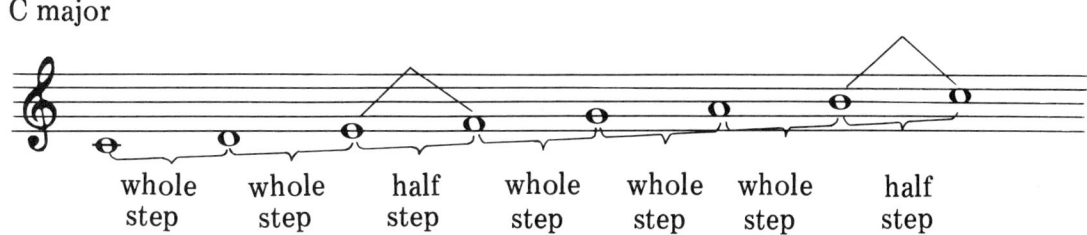

Natural or Normal Minor

Dorian
  or
Melodic - minor - 6th and 7th raised going up and lowered coming down

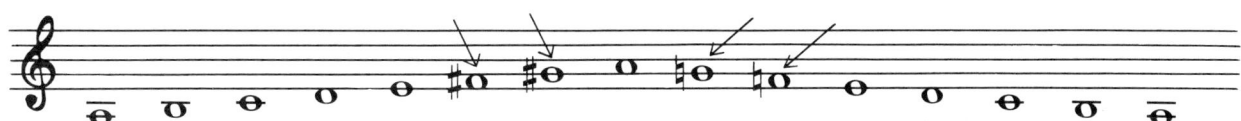

Harmonic minor 7th raised going up and coming down

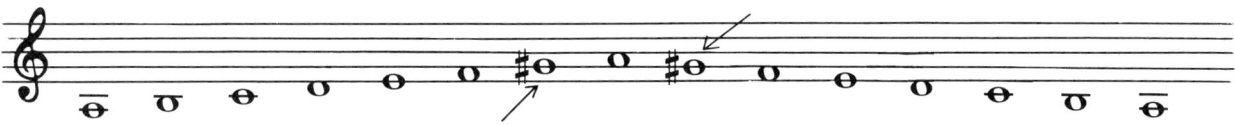

Hungarian - minor 4th and 7th raised going up and coming down

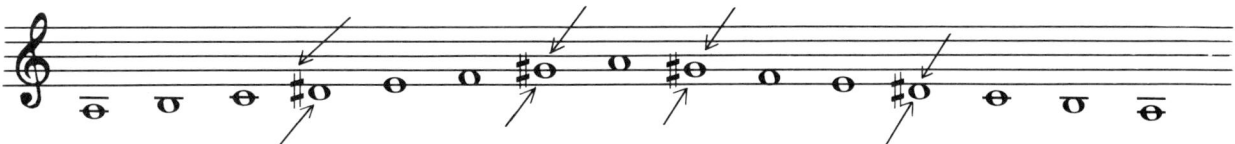

The most commonly used scales are the major, melodic and harmonic minor.

Scales - Continued

Degree-names of the scale ascending 1st-tonic - 2d supertonic - 3d - mediant - 4th sub-dominant - 5th dominant - 6th sub-mediant - 7th leading tone

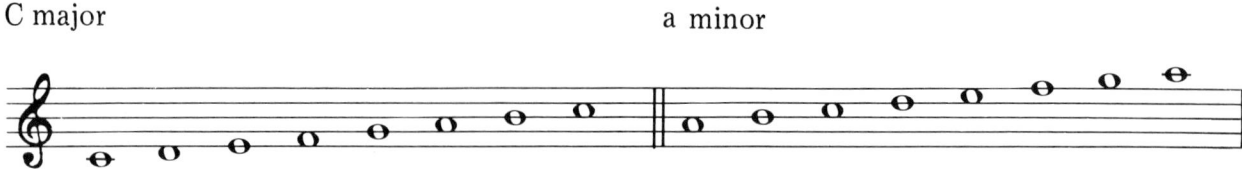

Scales are related when they have the same key signature.

Scales are parallel or unitonic - when they have the same tonic

A metrical measure is terminated by bars, and its contents governed by the time or motive signature. A rhythmical or grammatical measure is determined by its rhythmical contents, governed by the presence of a broken measure.

A whole rest ▬ is not a definite value like the others. It means a whole measure rest in every rhythm except 4/2 and 3/2.

Divertimento In D minor

Bb - major

G - melodic - minor

G - harmonic - minor

Moderato M.B.

Bravura

F. C. Z.

Tarantella

Rossini

Eb - major

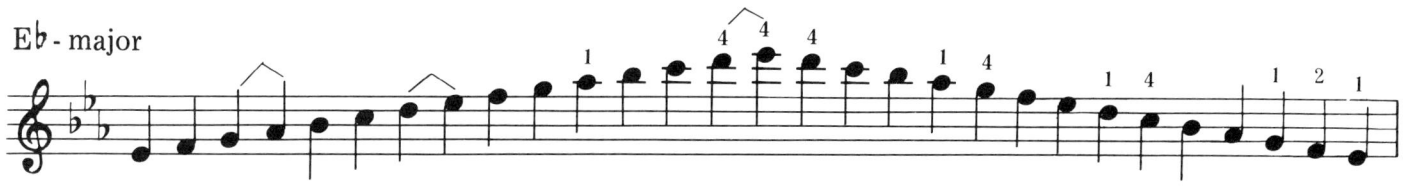

C - melodic - minor

C - harmonic - minor

F. C. Z.

Sonatina

Mysterioso

Ab major

F melodic minor

F harmonic minor

F. C. Z.

Estrinciendo

Danza

Con bizarria

F. C. Z.

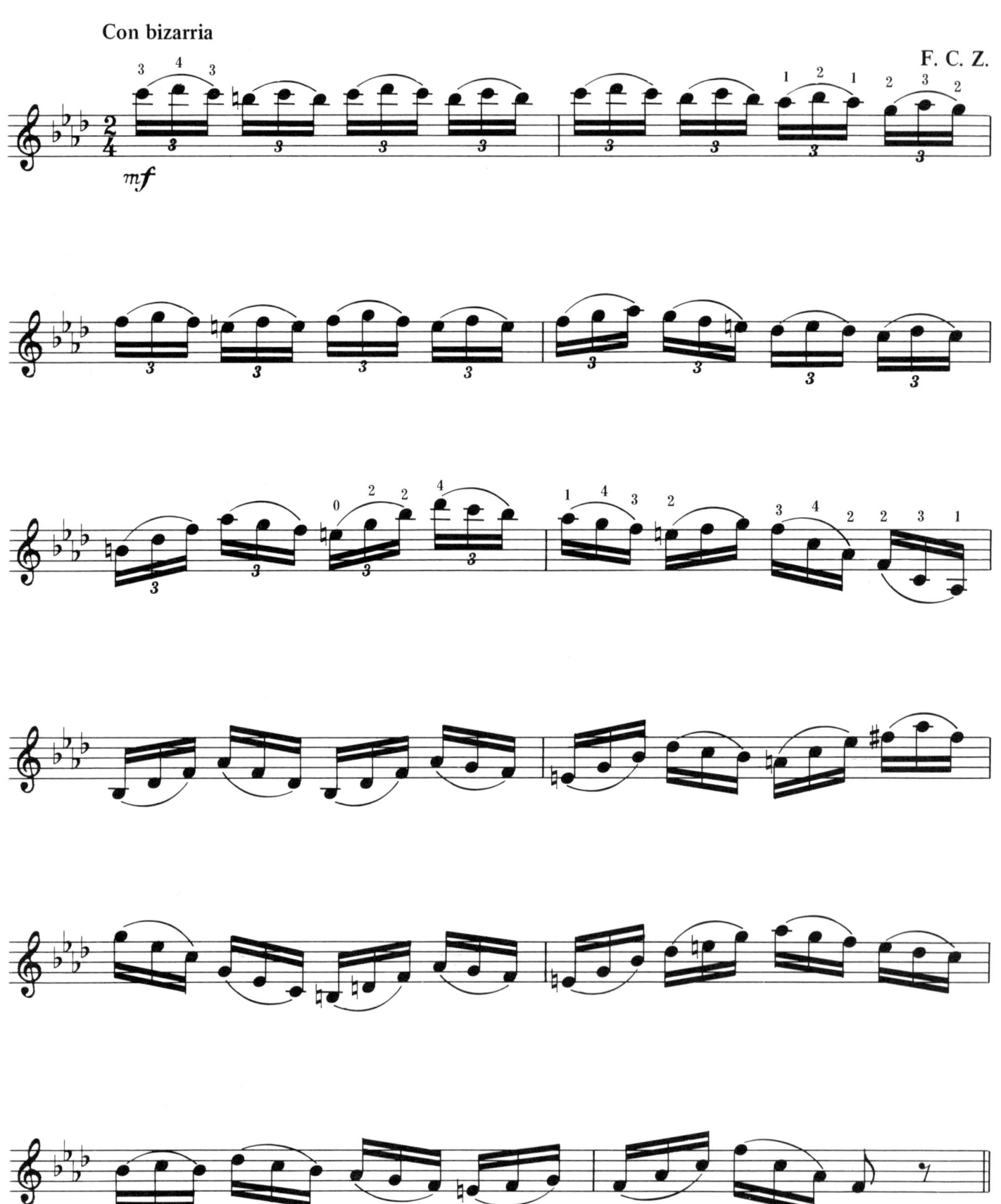

C Major

A - melodic - minor

A - harmonic - minor

F. C. Z.

This stroke must be made at the point with great firmness. All notes must have the same degree of force.

Martele (it) hammered - strongly marked

Cantabile - A minor

F. C. Z.

G major

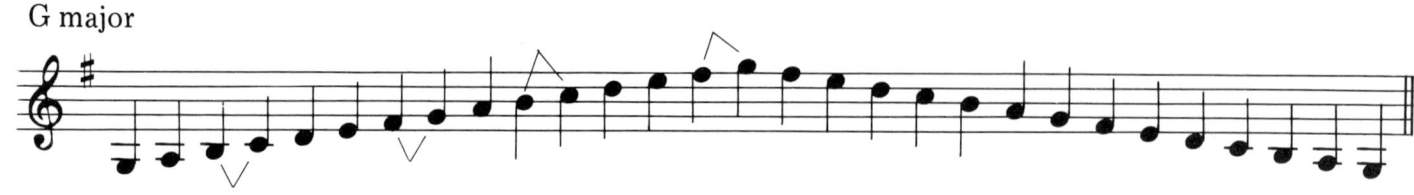

E melodic - minor

E - harmonic - minor

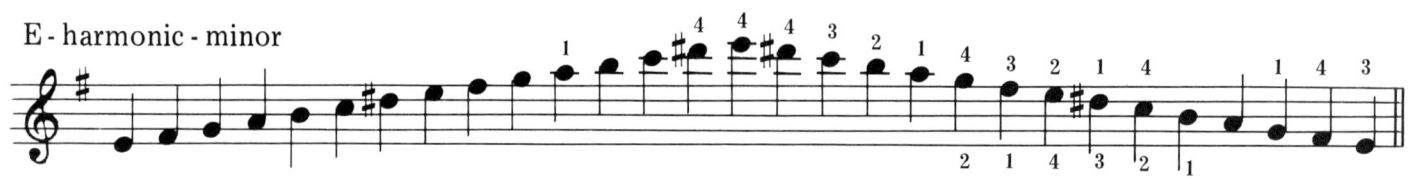

Retain - 3d - position

F. C. Z.

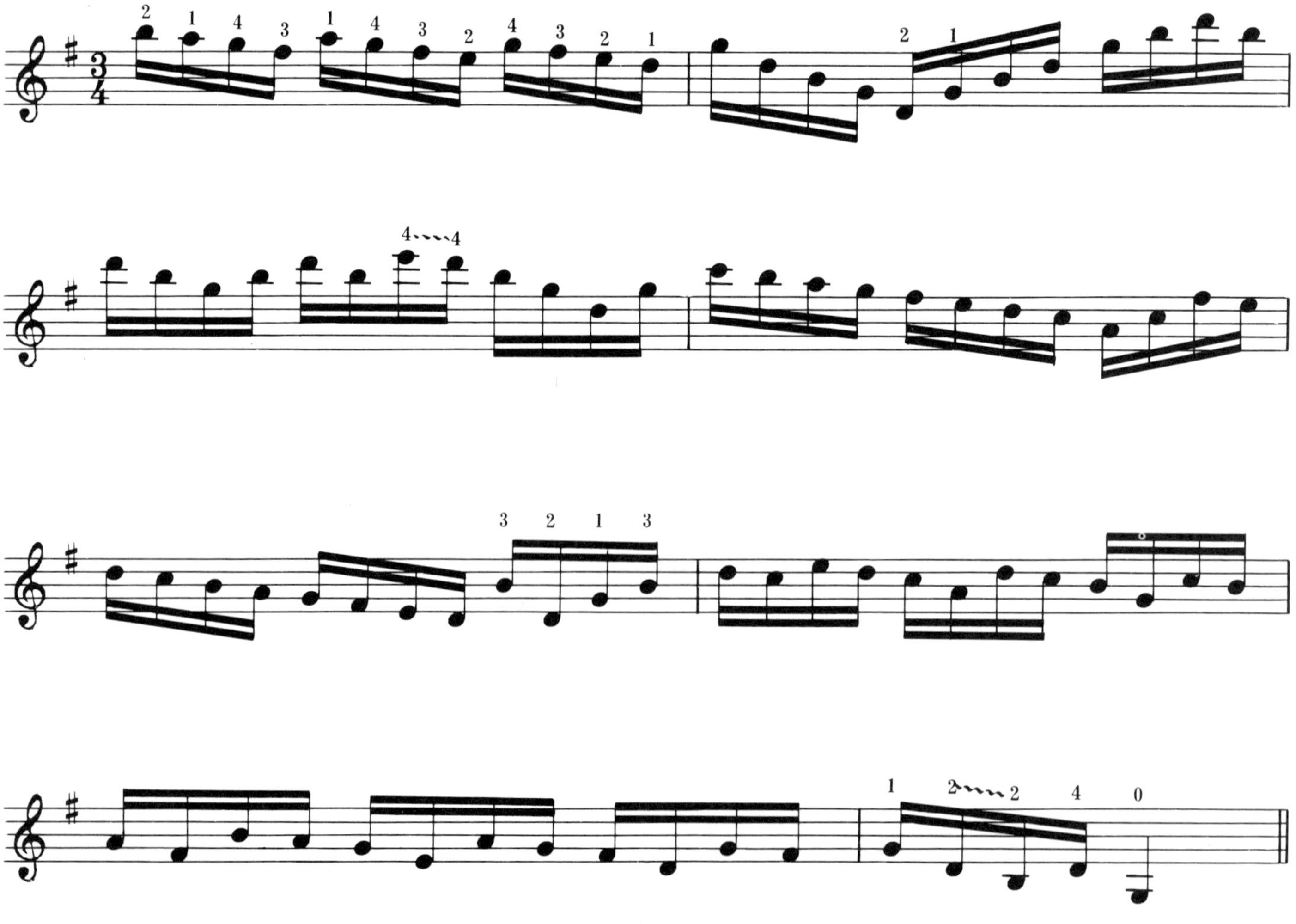

Calore

Cantinela

F. C. Z.

D major

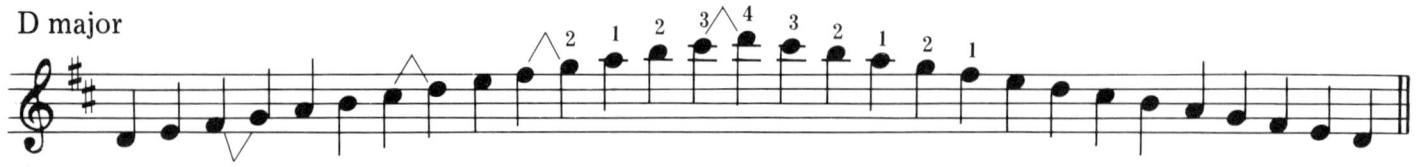

B melodic - minor

B - harmonic - minor

F. C. Z.

Etude In D Major

F. C. Z.

Grandioso

A major

F# melodic - minor

F# harmonic - minor

F. C. Z.

Prestézza

F. C. Z.

Molto Minore

F. C. Z.

E Major

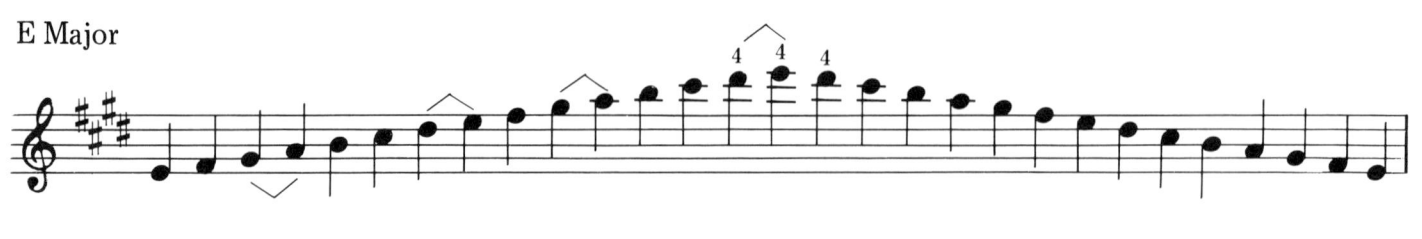

C# Melodic minor

C# Harmonic minor

Etude

F. C. Z.

Virtuoso

F. C. Z.

Mozart. number - 40 from Symphony in G minor.

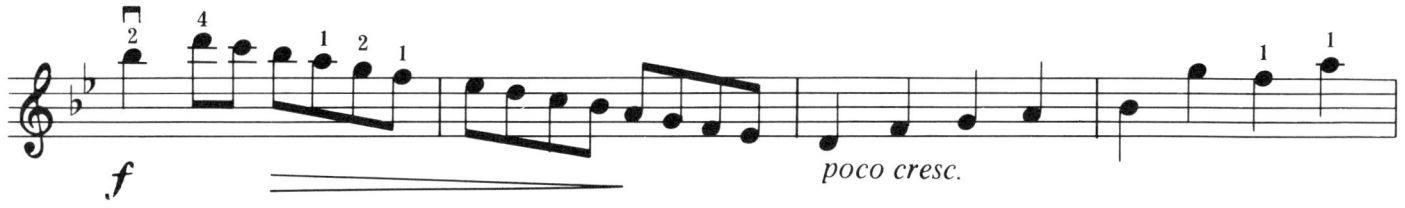

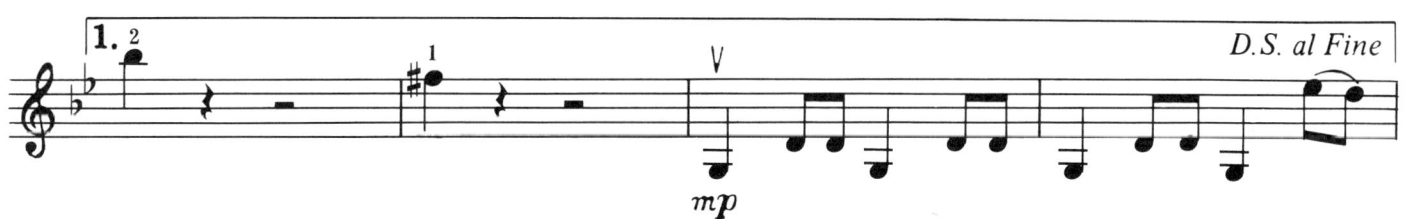

Mozart-Eine-Kleine-Nacht-Musik-

I

The 𝄴 comes to us from the middle ages. It was written by the monks in this manner (o). It later was changed to 𝄵 which we still use today to represent 4/4 rhythm.

Moderato contabile F. C. Z.

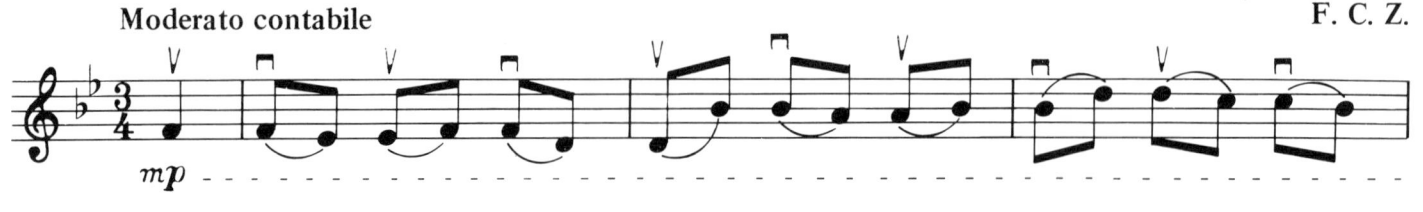

Sonatina

F. C. Z.

Bolero

Octave Studies

More Octaves

Some chief terms used for speed (slowest to the quickest).

Grave - slowest tempo in music
Largo - also slow and solemn
Adagio - quicker than largo
Andante (means going faster than - adagio)
(Moderato - in moderate - time)
(Allegretto - light - cheerful)
Allegro - quick lively faster than allegretto
Presto - rapidly, quickly

Valse-chromatic

Some Patterns In Syncopation

The Bow

An instrument made of lance wood or snake wood and horse hair. It was probably first used in ancient India or China towards the end of the 18th century. Francois Tourte brougt the bow to perfection. The present length of the bow is from 27 to 30 inches. The nut is made of ivory, ebony, or tortoise shell.

A Variety Of Sixths

The above intervals (6ths) should be practiced very slowly - intonation is very important.

Scales in Thirds   Melodic Form

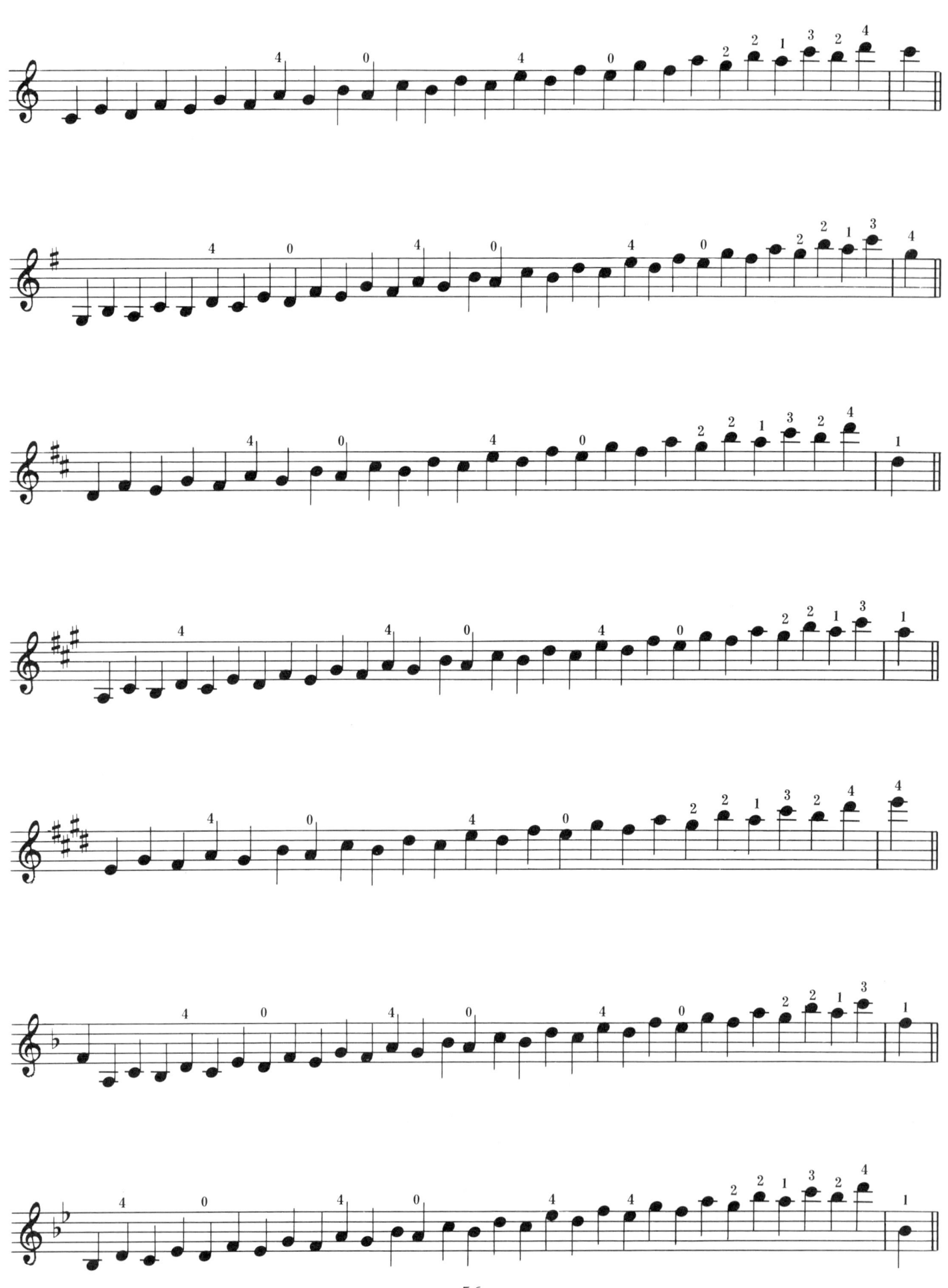

Thirds Continued

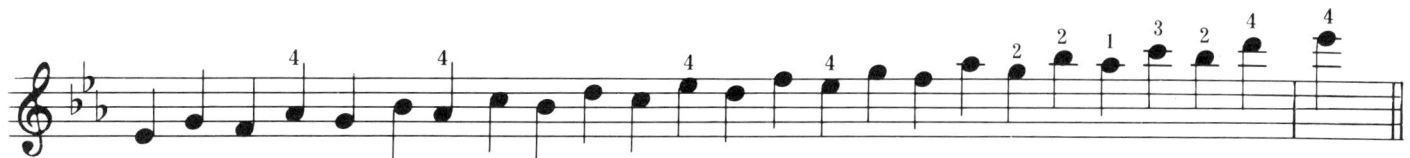

Scales in thirds in harmonic form accompanied by a short - melody

C major

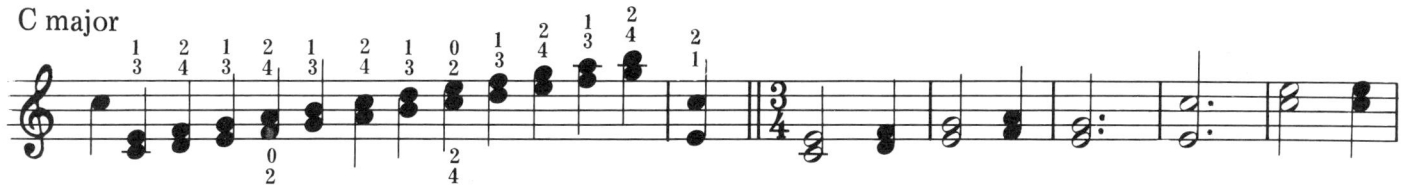

G major

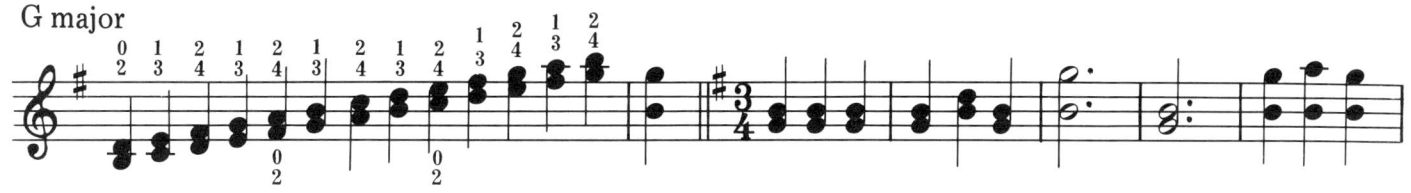

Caprice

F. C. Z.

Expression marks -
Amorosa - with tenderness and affection
Cantabile - in singing style - gracefull full of expression
Expressivo - played with espression.
Scherzo - played in sportive character. The scherzo was established by Beethoven as a symphonic move-
    ment.

Stück

Allegro - moderato

F. C. Z.

Deceptive

Montiverde

F. C. Z.

Pizzicato as well as tremolo on the violin is credited to Monteverde (1643)